ANIMAL STRENGTH AND COMBAT SPORTS

Isabel Thomas

D0177194

90710 000 298 742

Raintree is an imprint of Capstone Global Library Limited, a company incorporated in England and Wales having its registered office at 264 Banbury Road, Oxford OX2 7DY – Registered company number: 6695582

www.raintree.co.uk
myorders@raintree.co.uk

Text © Capstone Global Library Limited 2016
First published in hardback in 2016
Paperback edition first published in 2017
The moral rights of the proprietor have been asserted.

All rights reserved. No part of this publication may be reproduced in any form or by any means (including photocopying or storing it in any medium by electronic means and whether or not transiently or incidentally to some other use of this publication) without the written permission of the copyright owner, except in accordance with the provisions of the Copyright, Designs and Patents Act 1988 or under the terms of a licence issued by the Copyright Licensing Agency, Saffron House, 6–10 Kirby Street, London EC1N 8TS (www.cla.co.uk). Applications for the copyright owner's written permission should be addressed to the publisher.

Edited by Linda Staniford
Designed by Steve Mead
Picture research by Kelly Garvin
Production by Victoria Fitzgerald
Originated by Capstone Global Library Ltd
Printed and bound in China

ISBN 978 1 474 71360 3 (hardback)
19 18 17 16 15
10 9 8 7 6 5 4 3 2 1

ISBN 978 1 474 71369 6 (paperback)
20 19 18 17 16
10 9 8 7 6 5 4 3 2 1

British Library Cataloguing in Publication Data
A full catalogue record for this book is available from the British Library.

London Borough of Richmond Upon Thames

RTR DISCARDED

90710 000 298 742

FROM

Askews & Holts

RICHMOND UPON THAMES

J591.4 THO JUNIOR NON   £8.99

LIBRARY SERVICE 9781474713696

Acknowledgements
We would like to thank the following for permission to reproduce photographs:
Getty Image: Mark Ralston/AFP, 27; iStockphoto/NatureDisplay, 12, 31; Minden Pictures: Jez Bennett/NIS, 7, Mitsuaki Iwago, 5; Nature Picture Library/Nick Garbutt, 8; Newscom: Chuck Myers/MCT, 10, David Fleetham-VWPics, 17, Donald M. Jones/Minden Pictures, 11, Frans Lanting/Mint Images, 24, George Bernard/Evolve/Photoshot, 25, Harry E. Walker/MCT, 6, Jonathan Brady/EPA, 22, Lindsey Parnaby/EPA, 4, Neil Munns/EPA, 18, Sportsphoto/Splash News, 14, Stephen Dalton/Minden Pictures, 21, Vince Burton/NHPA/Photoshot, 16; Science Source/Anthony Mercieca, 23; Shutterstock: Adrov Andriy, cover (top left), Dr. Morley Read, 9, LauraD, 19 (inset), MarcusVDT, cover (top right), sevenke, cover (bottom), Stuart G. Porter, 20, wonderisland, 13; Superstock: Animals Animals, 19, Tier und Naturfotografie, 15

Design elements: Elena Paletskaya, kavalenkava volha, La Gorda, Nikiteev_Konstantin, PinkPueblo, Potapov Alexander, yyang

We would like to thank Michael Bright for his help in the preparation of this book.

Every effort has been made to contact copyright holders of material reproduced in this book. Any omissions will be rectified in subsequent printings if notice is given to the publisher.

All the internet addresses (URLs) given in this book were valid at the time of going to press. However, due to the dynamic nature of the internet, some addresses may have changed, or sites may have changed or ceased to exist since publication. While the author and publisher regret any inconvenience this may cause readers, no responsibility for any such changes can be accepted by either the author or the publisher.

Key

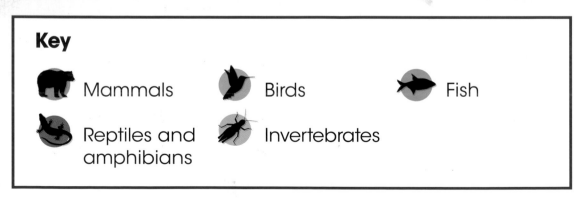

Mammals

Birds

Fish

Reptiles and amphibians

Invertebrates

CONTENTS

Some words are shown in bold, **like this**. You can find out what they mean by looking in the glossary.

LET THE GAMES BEGIN!

The world's best sportspeople come together every four years, to compete at the Olympic Games. Weightlifting, combat and archery events test their skill, strength and **endurance**.

In any forest, ocean or grassland, you'll find animals that could beat the best human athletes. Super strength, fighting skills and a great aim are all **adaptations** that help animals to **survive**. Let's find out which animal athletes deserve a medal at the Animalympics!

WEIGHTLIFTING

Olympic weightlifters must heave a **barbell** above their head. If their body moves or their arms bend, the lift does not count! The strongest **competitors** can lift more than 260 kilograms (573 pounds) – the weight of three average-sized adults!

steel bar

barbell

heavy disc

🐘 Elephant

Elephants don't need two arms to lift heavy weights – just one trunk! The muscles in the trunk allow elephants to tear down trees to get to the juicy leaves at the top. With the help of their tusks, African elephants can carry up to **300 kilograms (660 pounds)**, snatching bronze!

trunk

Harpy eagle

Lifting your own body weight is impressive, but flying with it is a real test of strength! Harpy eagles pluck 8-kilogram (18-pound) sloths and monkeys from trees, and carry them to a place where they can feast in peace.

wing muscles have to work harder

thick legs

powerful talons

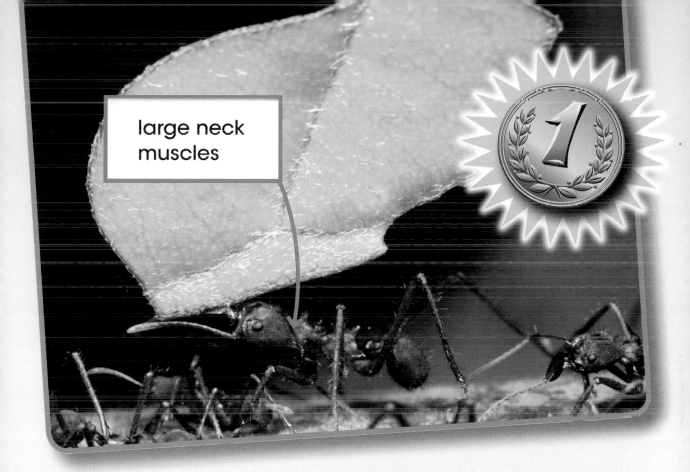

large neck muscles

 Ant

Weightlifters compete against rivals of the same size and weight. Scientists compare animal strength by looking at how much they can lift for their size. Olympians can lift up to three times their own weight, but some ants can walk along carrying leaves or **prey** more than 50 times heavier than themselves!

FENCING

Fencing champions battle with thin, bendy swords. To score a point, they must touch their opponent's body with the pointed tip of their blade. The best fencers have great balance and quick reactions.

hand guard

chest guard

wire mask to protect face

American elk

Every year, in late summer, male American elk (or wapiti) lock antlers in a battle to decide who becomes the boss of each herd. The strongest deer usually wins.

Antlers are six times tougher than normal bones. They fall off and grow back every year.

Hummingbirds

Hummingbirds may look pretty and dainty, but they are fearsome fighters! Males have long bills which they use like swords. They go head to head in competition, stabbing rivals in the throat to defend the area where they feed.

Bills have sharp tips.

Rhinoceros beetle

Male Rhinoceros beetles use their long horns to prise other males off the best branches. This helps them to win the best food, and the best chance of mating with females. Each type of Rhinoceros beetle has horns specially adapted to their fighting moves, winning them gold in the fencing event.

Horns are long but light.

BOXING

Olympic boxers are strong and fast. They score points by hitting their opponent's head or upper body with their gloves. Boxers are not allowed to hit "below the belt" – a line level with their belly button.

headguard

boxing glove

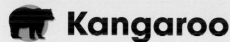 Kangaroo

Kangaroos are famous for their boxing **bouts**. As with other animals, most fights are about winning the right to mate. Kangaroos scuffle as they try to grip their opponent's shoulders and deliver a hard kick in the belly. This breaks the rules of boxing, so kangaroos would be disqualified – they finish in third place!

sharp claws

large shoulder muscles

 # Hares

Human boxers are always matched by size and gender. But brown hare boxing matches are boys versus girls! Before they are ready to mate, female hares defend themselves from aggressive males. The hares stand on their hind legs and attack each other with their front paws.

female hare (jill)

male hare (jack)

2

You can spot these boxing matches all through the spring and summer. Hares have up to four **litters** a year.

Mantis shrimp

Boxers must move quickly to land and avoid punches. The animal with the fastest punch of all is the peacock mantis shrimp. It swings its hammer-like claw fast enough to heat the water nearby! Mantis shrimps use these powerful punches to crush the shells of snail **prey**.

This part swings forwards.

ARCHERY

Olympic archers shoot arrows at a target 70 metres (230 feet) away. From this distance, the target looks smaller than a drawing pin. The winner is the archer that gets his or her arrows closest to the centre of the target.

bow

arrow

Feathers help the arrow fly straight.

The judges have to use a telescope to read each archer's score!

Cone snail

How dangerous is a snail? Deadly, when it's armed with a **harpoon**! The cone snail lives in coral reefs. When it gets close to its **prey**, it fires a harpoon loaded with **venom**. The fish becomes motionless, and can be gobbled up whole.

Cone snails only take the bronze because they have to be right next to their target.

The cone snail fires its harpoon from this tube.

Spitting cobra

Spitting cobras defend themselves from larger animals by shooting stinging **venom** at their attackers' eyes. These snakes are brilliant at hitting even moving targets.

can spit more than 1.5 metres (5 feet)

A scientist hid behind a sheet of plastic and let cobras spit at his eyes. He found their aim was perfect nine out of ten times!

Archerfish

These fish are so good at archery, they are even named after the sport. Archerfish use their mouths as water pistols, shooting jets of water to knock insects into the water. This **adaptation** helps them catch **prey** that other fish can't reach.

insect prey

By changing the shape of their mouths, archerfish control the speed and shape of the water jet to match the distance to their target.

WRESTLING

In Olympic matches, wrestlers battle for two minutes at a time. They score points by throwing their opponent to the ground, or holding them so they can't move. A wrestler automatically wins if she manages to pin her opponent's shoulders to the ground.

wrestling mat

Cave paintings show that wrestling is a 5,000 year-old sport!

Rattlesnake

Male rattlesnakes fight to win the chance to breed with females. They could kill each other with deadly bites, but they have adapted to wrestle instead. These matches test the snakes' strength while avoiding serious injuries.

The match ends when the weaker snake slinks off.

Brown bears

Male brown bears are fearsome wrestlers. When they fight over food or **territory**, their sharp teeth and claws can cause serious injuries. To avoid this, brown bears have other ways of showing how big and strong they are. Standing on their hind legs and roaring is often enough to frighten a smaller bear away.

Strawberry poison dart frogs

When male Strawberry poison dart frogs croak, they are telling other frogs, "This is my territory". If another male dares to answer, the frogs wrestle to find out who gets to stay. Fights last up to 20 minutes, ending when one frog gets pinned down – just like in the Olympics!

AMAZING ADAPTATIONS

Animals don't lift heavy weights, wrestle or aim well for sport. The body features and behaviour that make animals good at lifting, fighting or aiming are **adaptations** that help them **survive** in certain **habitats**.

Strength and fighting skills help animals to find food, attract mates, look after their young or avoid getting eaten. This means these features will get passed on to the next generation.

Watching record-breaking animal athletes helps scientists find out how animal bodies work. This information is used in amazing ways, such as designing robots that carry objects using as little energy as possible.

This robot is designed like a cheetah. It can run at speeds of up to 45 kilometres (28.3 miles) per hour.

MEDAL TABLE

It's time for the Animalympic medal ceremony! The animal kingdom is divided into groups. Animals with similar features belong to the same class. Which class will take home the most medals for strength and combat sports?

Mammals

Mammals are warm-blooded animals with hair or fur. Mother mammals make milk to feed their babies. They live on the land and in water.

Reptiles and amphibians

Reptiles and amphibians are cold-blooded animals. Reptiles have dry, scaly skin. Amphibians have moist, smooth skin.

Birds

Birds have feathers, wings, and a beak. They can live on land or at sea, but not permanently underwater.

Invertebrates

This group includes all animals without a backbone, such as insects, spiders and snails. Many have a skeleton on the outside of their bodies instead.

Fish

Fish live in salt water or fresh water. They have fins for swimming, and gills to breathe underwater.

RESULTS

EVENT	③ BRONZE	② SILVER	① GOLD
WEIGHTLIFTING	Elephant	Harpy Eagle	Ant
FENCING	American elk or wapiti	Hummingbird	Rhinoceros beetle
BOXING	Kangaroo	Hare	Mantis shrimp
ARCHERY	Cone snail	Spitting cobra	Archerfish
WRESTLING	Rattlesnake	Brown bear	Strawberry poison dart frog

ANIMAL	RANK	GOLD	SILVER	BRONZE
Invertebrates	1	①①①	②②	③
Mammals	2		②②	③③③
Birds	3		②	
Reptiles and amphibians	4	①		③
Fish	5	①		

GLOSSARY

adaptation change to the body, workings or behaviour of a living thing that makes it better suited to its habitat

barbell long metal bar used in weightlifting; weights are added at each end

bout wrestling or boxing match

competitor person taking part in a sporting match or contest

endurance a person or animal's ability to continue doing something without giving up, even when it is very difficult

habitat place where a plant or animal lives

harpoon spear with barbs, that is jabbed, fired or thrown at a target

litter group of young animals born to the same animal at the same time

prey animal that is hunted and killed by another animal, for food

survive stay alive

territory area of land defended by an animal or group of animals

venom poison made by an animal

FIND OUT MORE

Books
Horrible Science: Evolve or Die, Phil Gates and Tony De Saulles (Scholastic, 2008)

Amazing Animal Adaptations series, Julie Murphy (Raintree, 2012)

Combat Sports: Boxing, Paul Mason (Franklin Watts, 2012)

Websites
Find out about Olympic weightlifting, fencing, boxing, archery and wrestling at:
http://www.olympic.org/sports

Find out how to get involved in archery at:
http://www.archerygb.org/1659.php

Find out about wrestling for schools at:
http://www.britishwrestling.org/page.

INDEX